snoo

facts & fun book about planes

ABRIDGED EDITION

**Based on the
Charles M. Schulz Characters**

Happy House Books

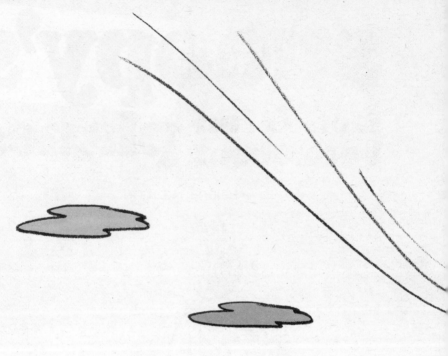

Designed by Terry Flanagan

Many of the first airplanes had two or three sets of wings!

An engine makes an airplane go. For takeoff and for landing, an airplane needs landing gear with wheels.

The pilot sits in the cockpit and flies the airplane. Sometimes a copilot helps.

The cockpit has a lot of instruments in it. They show the pilot exactly how high the airplane is flying and how fast it is going.

An airport is a very busy place! It has
many runways. When a plane takes off, it
speeds along a runway until it is moving fast
enough to lift up...up...up into the air.

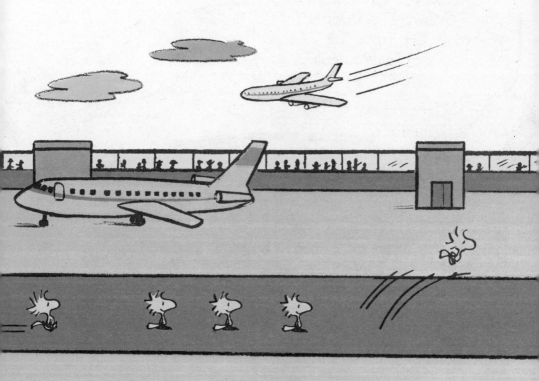

In the airport's control tower, air-traffic controllers use two-way radios to tell pilots where to land and take off. The controllers make sure every plane is flying safely.

An aircraft carrier is like a floating airport. The ship's large, flat deck is the runway.

A seaplane lands right on the water of the ocean or a lake. It takes off from the water, too. A seaplane has floats instead of wheels.

Amphibians are airplanes that can land on water or on land. In the water the plane's body floats like a boat, but it also has wheels that pop out for landing on solid ground.

In places that have a lot of snow on the ground, people fly airplanes that have skis instead of wheels for landing!

A glider is an airplane without an engine!
A plane WITH an engine pulls the glider high
into the sky, then lets the glider go. The
glider rides on gusts of wind. A cloth tube
called a windsock fills with air and shows the
pilot which way the wind is blowing.

Helicopters have no wings, but they have blades on top that whirl around and around. That's why they are sometimes called WHIRLYBIRDS.

Helicopters can fly forward, backward, and straight up and down, too. Or they can stay in the air without moving. Helicopters are good for rescuing people in trouble.

VTOLs are another kind of airplane that fly straight up and down. But they have wings, and they can fly faster than helicopters. VTOL stands for Vertical Take-Off and Landing.

Crop-dusting planes swoop low over farm fields. They spray the fields with plant food and bug killers to keep the plants healthy.

Sound travels very fast. But supersonic
airplanes can fly FASTER than sound!

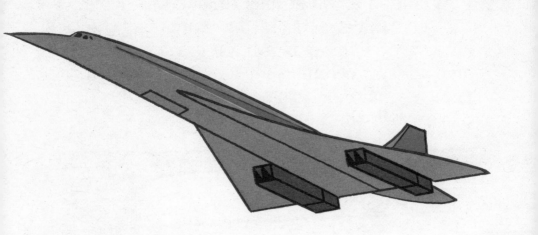

When an airplane has finished its work, the pilot takes it back to a hangar at the airport. A hangar is a huge garage for airplanes. Mechanics check every part of the plane — making sure that it's all ready for more work the next day.